This book is gifted

_____

On the occasion of:

_____

With love from:

_____

"Every good and every perfect gift is from God"
(James 1:17).

But First, Let's Say Our Prayers
Learning to Pray Before Bed

Corey L. Richards

Illustrated by C. Blackwell

Published by Prayer, Faith, and Love LLC

But First, Let's Say Our Prayers
Learning to Pray Before Bed

Published by Prayer, Faith, and Love, LLC
Chesterfield, MI 48051

Library of Congress Control Number: 2020916094
ISBN 978-1-7355839-0-7 (Hardcover)
ISBN 978-1-7355839-1-4 (Ebook)

To Abby and Jacob, who motivate me daily
to live and love like Jesus –

You will never go wrong obeying the Bible.

I love you both to the moon and back,
a million, trillion times.

Mom

It is time for bed.
It is time to pray.
Let's tell God "thanks" while
we remember our day.

First, get on our knees and bow our heads,
then press our hands together, our fingers not spread.

We'll count up our blessings one by one
and praise God for all the good things He's done.

Did He answer your prayer and your wish came true?
For these types of things, we should say, "thank you."

Then after that, we admit our mistakes.
A simple "I'm sorry" is all that it takes.

Did you LIE about something?

Did you FIGHT with your brother?

Did you do something SNEAKY

or HURT one another?

Make sure you're honest when talking to Jesus.
His love is so big, He will always forgive us.

I'm sorry I lied to Dad today and that I blamed my little brother

please forgive me because i took a cookie when Grandma wasnt looking

Dear God, Please Forgive Us when we Fought With each other

I'm sorry I hurt Sara When we were playing Basktball. I hope she feels better

The last thing we do is tell Him our concerns and our fears
so our joy will return, and our worries will disappear.

Is there a meanie at school
who you wish would be nice,

or a problem at home
where you need some advice?

Did your friend move away, and now you feel alone?

Or do you have big, big dreams that aren't yet quite known?

Whatever your problem, let God know it all.
No problem is too big, and no problem is too small!

Try to talk to God at least once a day,
but talk more if you can—He loves when you pray!

After you pray, take some time
to be still.
Be patient and let God show
you His will.

Don't lose faith if He doesn't answer right away.
He will in the perfect time, in the most perfect way.

As you wait for the answers to all of your prayers,
remember the ways God has shown you He cares!

Goodnight, my sweet child, let the Lord give you rest.
Sleep tonight knowing you are loved and are blessed.

When you wake up tomorrow, give thanks for God's Word.
He is faithful. He is strong. And He is so, so, SO good!

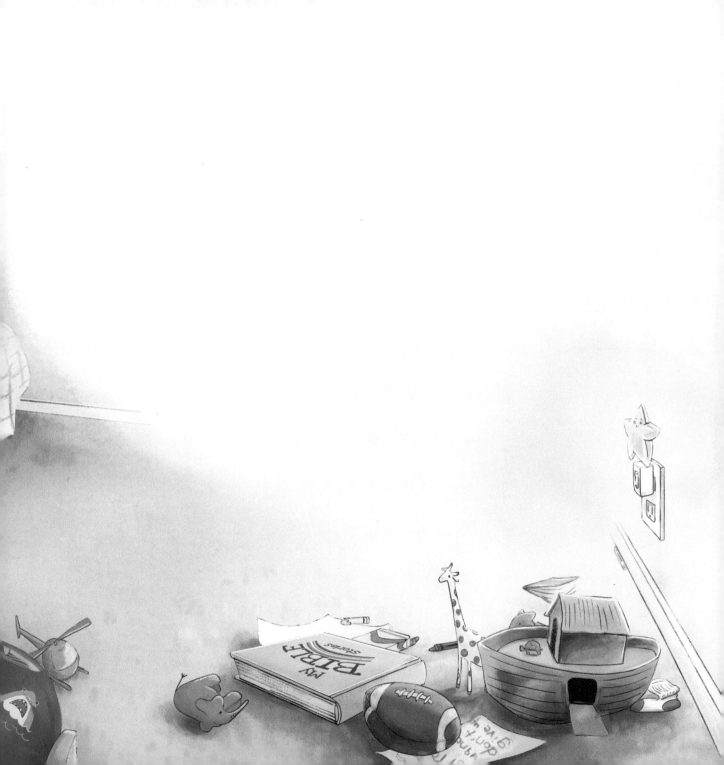

"Always be joyful. Never stop praying. Give thanks no matter what happens. God wants you to thank him because you believe in Christ Jesus" (1 Thessalonians 5:16-18).

Note to the Adult Reader

No matter our age, gender, or background, we all need God in our life. I hope this book will help you start, or perhaps continue, your journey of encouraging your child(ren) to develop an intimate, personal relationship with God through prayer. The sooner they develop that relationship, the earlier they will be able to recognize and reject views and opinions that conflict with the truths and promises He offers.

I encourage you to have a conversation with your children about "why" we pray. Prayer gives us a chance to spend time with God and to reflect on our day in terms of what went wrong, what went right, and where we can use His help and advice. The more we live by His Word and put it into practice, the more we can trust that when it rains, and the water rises, our house will not fall (Matthew 7:24-27).

Please assure your precious little one that their prayers, much like themselves, do not have to be perfect. When they do not know the right words to pray, remind them that God knows what they need even before they ask (Matthew 6:8). Reassure them that God will answer their prayers (Isaiah 49:8) at the right time and in the perfect way. Sometimes He does not respond in the way we want, and sometimes His answer is "no" or "not yet," but that is because He is all-knowing. They must understand that it can take days or weeks or even longer for God to answer, though even in the silence, He is working.

The next page includes some bible verses for your child to memorize. Some ideas to help them learn the verses include:

- Read them aloud several times while they listen to you; have them repeat after you
- Write them on a separate piece of paper; consider having your child trace your words if necessary
- Imagine a scene representing the verse using your imaginations
- Turn them into a song together, using whatever melody comes to mind

Finally, there is also a page for your child to record their prayer requests, allowing them to later reflect on which ones, or how many, God has answered.

I pray that together we can raise our youngest generation believing that if they come near to God, He will come near to them (James 4:8).

P.S. I would love to hear how this book has positively touched you or your child's life. Please consider letting me know at https://CoreyLRichards.com.

Scriptures to Memorize:

"Do to others as you want them to do to you" (Luke 6:31).

"The Lord loves us very much" (Lamentations 3:22).

"Be kind...to one another. Forgive one another" (Ephesians 4:32).

"When I'm afraid, I put my trust in You" (Psalm 56:3).

"Always be joyful because you belong to the Lord.
I will say it again. Be joyful!" (Philippians 4:4).

"Love one another" (1 John 3:23).

"Lord, I will praise You with all my heart" (Psalm 138:1).

"Trust in the Lord with all your heart" (Proverbs 3:5).

"I can do all this by the power of Christ.
He gives me strength" (Philippians 4:13).

"Love your neighbor as you love yourself" (Matthew 22:39).

"Give thanks to the Lord, because He is good.
His faithful love continues forever" (Psalm 136:1).

"Do not be afraid for I am with you" (Isaiah 43:5).

"Obey everything I have commanded you.
And you can be sure that I am always with you,
to the very end" (Matthew 28:20).

"Children, obey your parents in everything.
That pleases the Lord" (Colossians 3:20).

"Every word of God is perfect. He is like a shield to
those who trust in him. He keeps them safe" (Proverbs 30:5).

"Think about things that are in heaven. Don't think about
things that are only on earth" (Colossians 3:2).

"Jesus Christ is the same yesterday, today and forever"
(Hebrews 13:8).

"The LORD is good to all" (Psalm 145:9).

"Everyone has sinned. No one measures up to God's glory"
(Romans 3:23).

Consider Recording Your Prayers

"Don't worry about anything. No matter what happens, tell God about everything. Ask and pray, and give thanks to Him" (Phillippians 4:6).

Date: Today I prayed for:

_____   _____

                          _____

_____   _____

                          _____

_____   _____

                          _____

_____   _____

                          _____

Date: Today I prayed for:

_____   _____

_____

_____   _____

_____

_____   _____

_____

_____   _____

_____

_____   _____

_____

About the Author:

Corey L. Richards lives in a fun, family-friendly neighborhood in Chesterfield, Michigan. She should feel like she has everything, but when she unexpectedly became a single mom, Corey struggled with life's demands. To keep it together, she began nurturing her relationship with God through prayer. With the goal of ensuring her children will have that same powerful tool to navigate their own lives, she sought to create a foundation of prayer for them, too.

It's not all serious business in the Richards' household. Corey's two elementary-aged children love to use their imagination. Although she's terrible at playing with dolls and building anything impressive with blocks, Corey loves board games and often breaks out into ridiculous song and dance which makes the kids squeal with laughter.

The family also enjoys going for walks, playing outside, and indulging in anything sweet. If it wasn't enough being a full-time, career-focused mom, Corey recently decided to pursue a second master's degree, this time from George Washington University Law School. So, while she'd like to say evenings find her cozied up at home with a journal, Bible, and chai tea—the truth is she's likely doing homework alongside her kids!

But First, Let's Say Our Prayers: Learning to Pray Before Bed is her debut book.

You can learn more by visiting https://CoreyLRichards.com.

CPSIA information can be obtained
at www.ICGtesting.com
Printed in the USA
LVHW072005260121
677518LV00014B/216